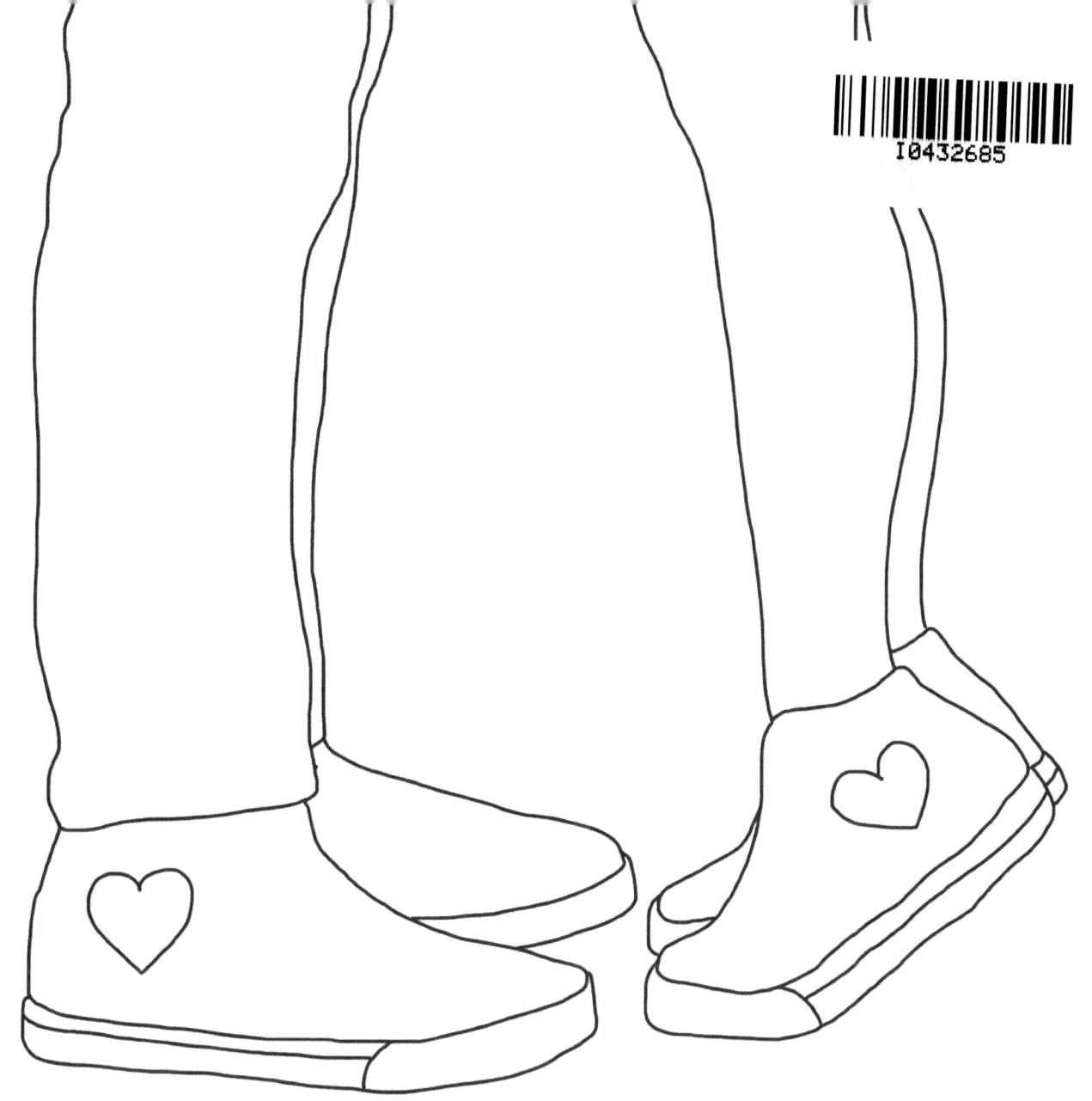

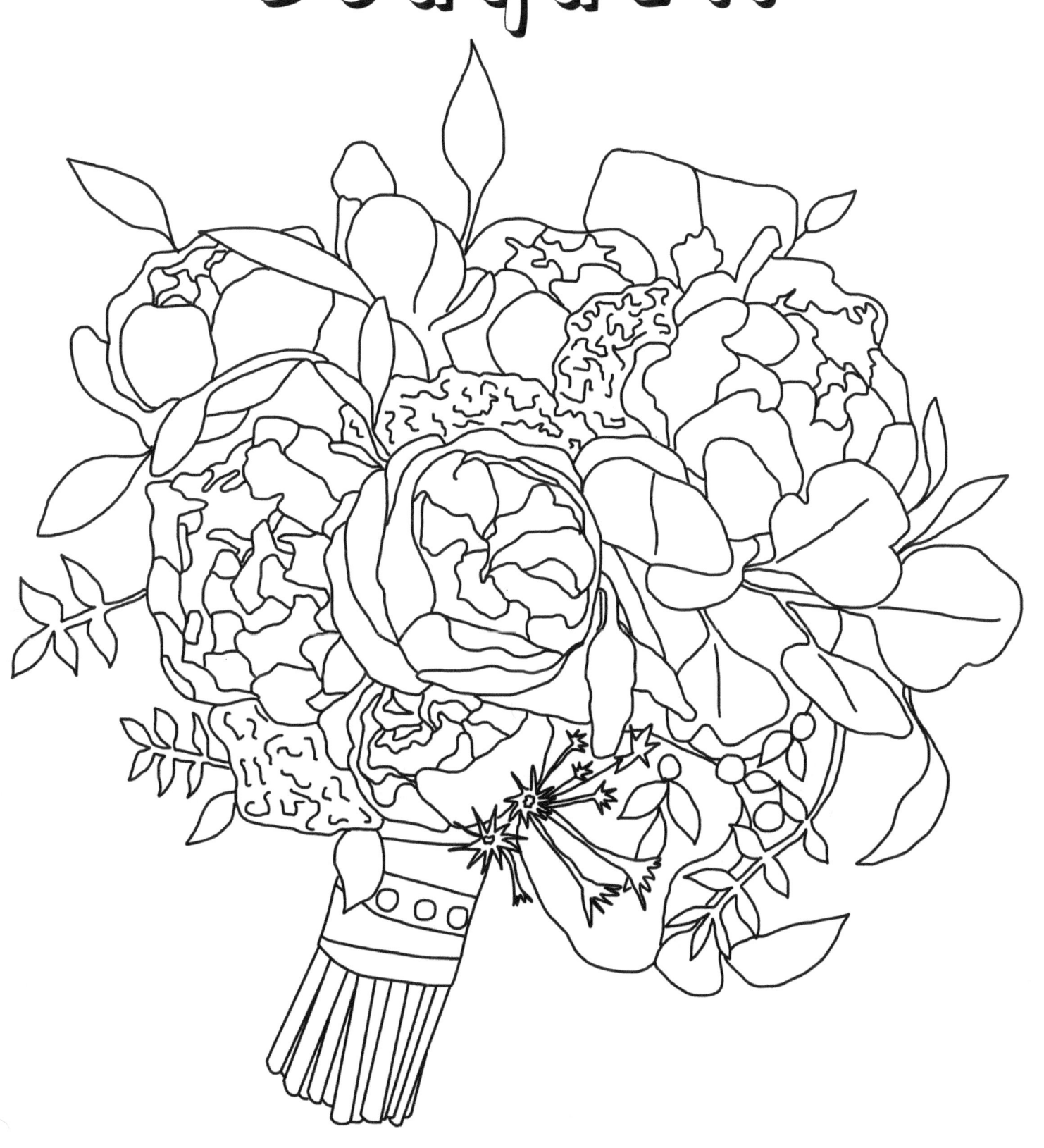

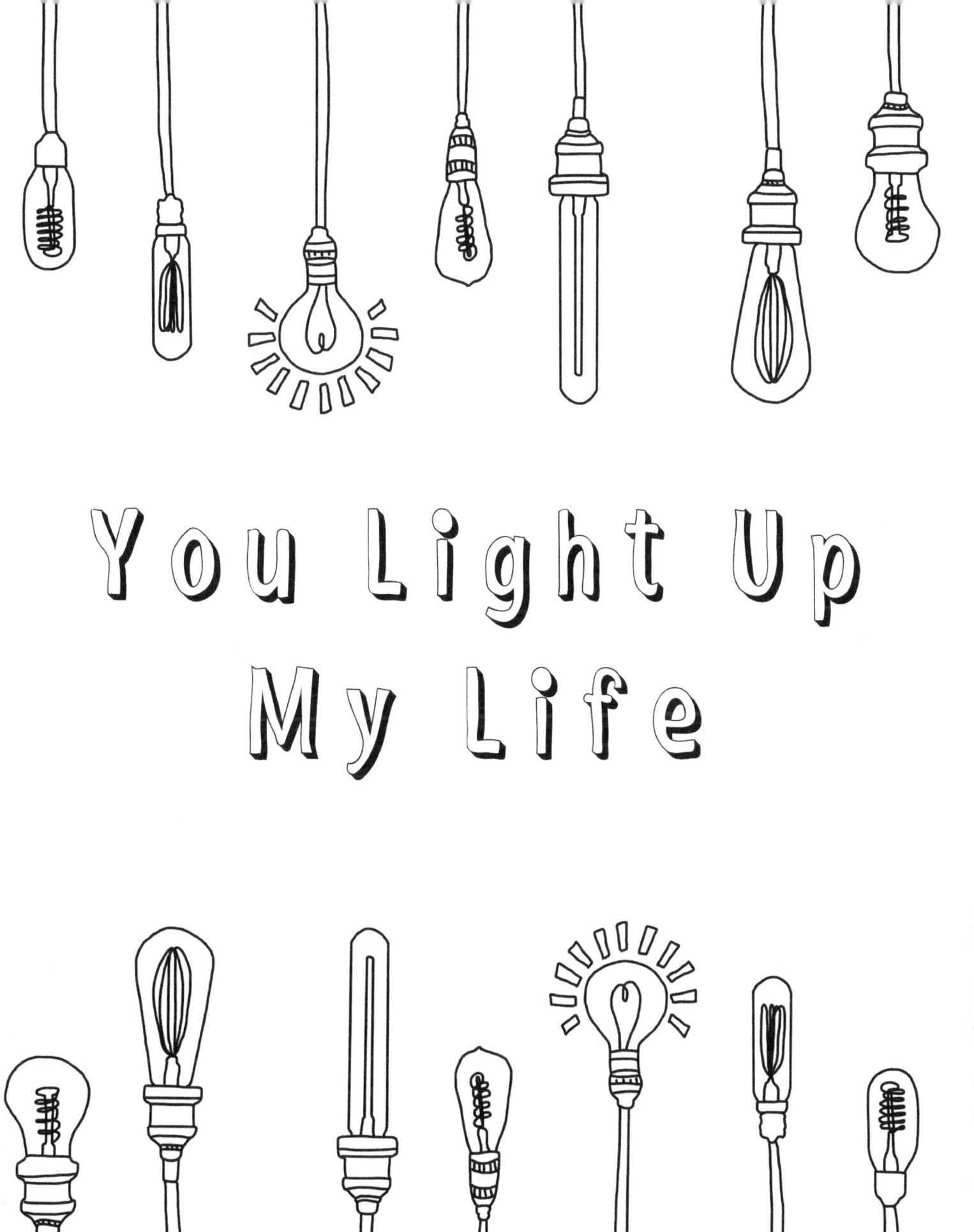

Color The Cake!

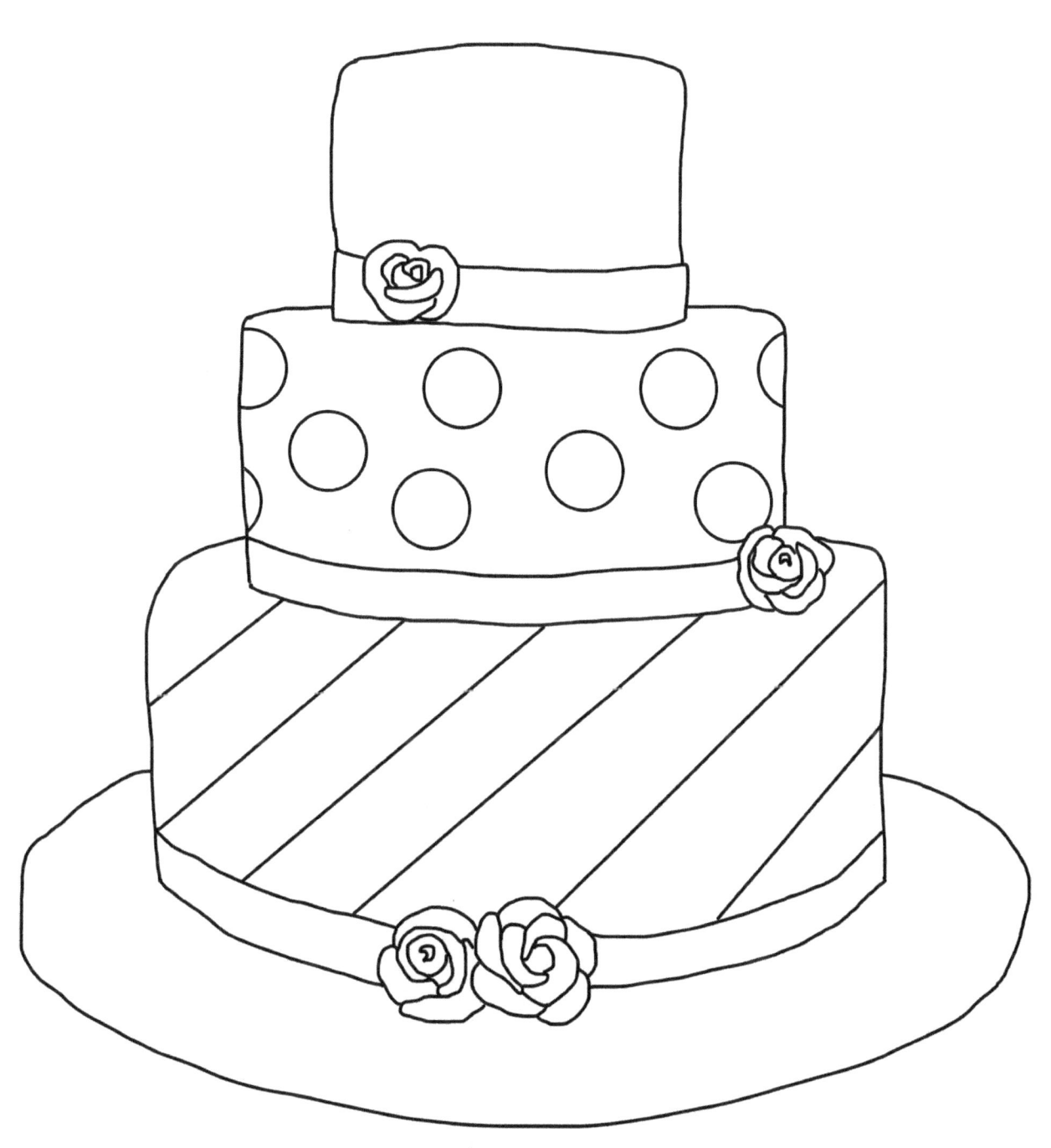

Design the Dress!

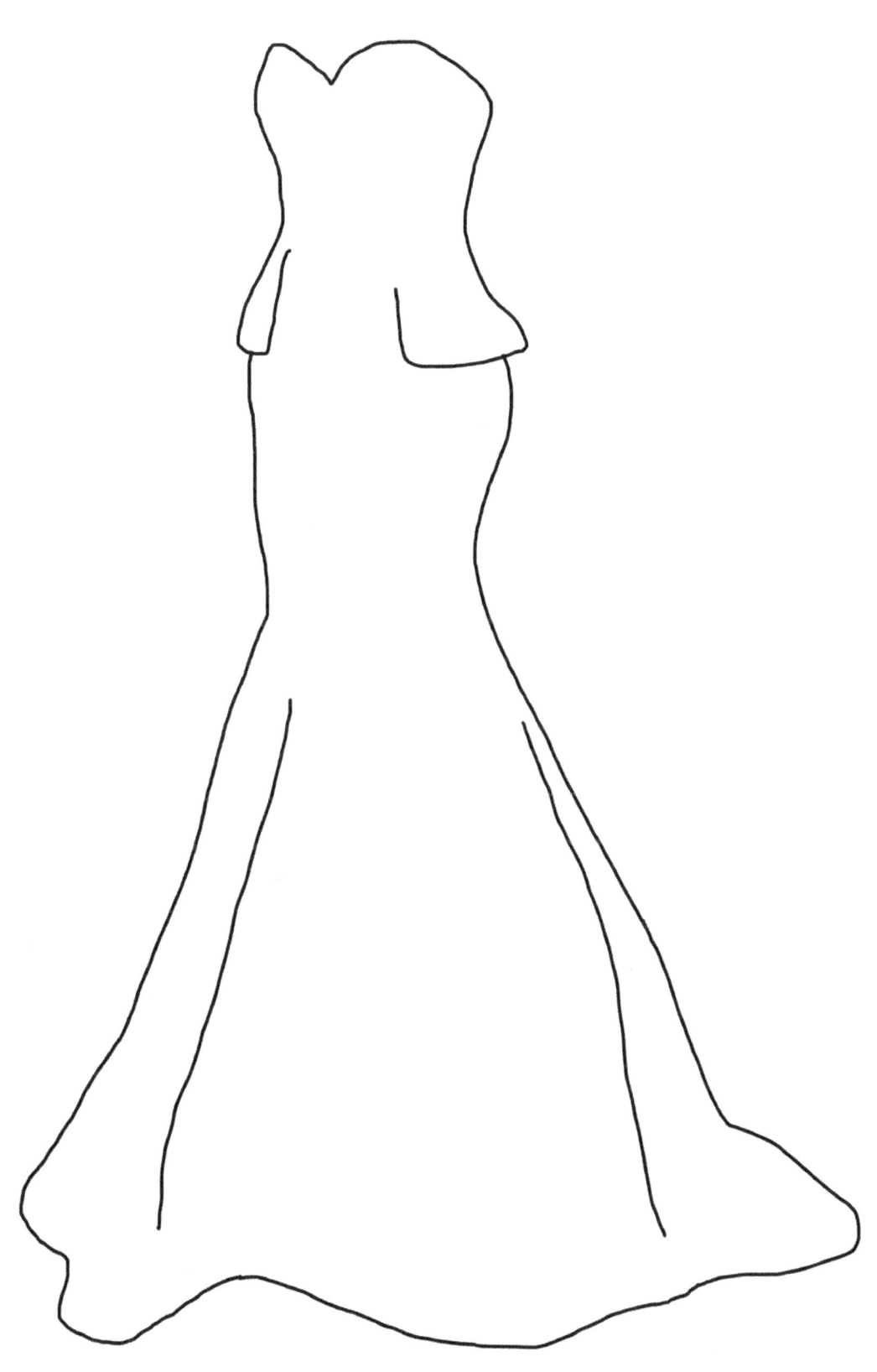

May Life Be Succulent!

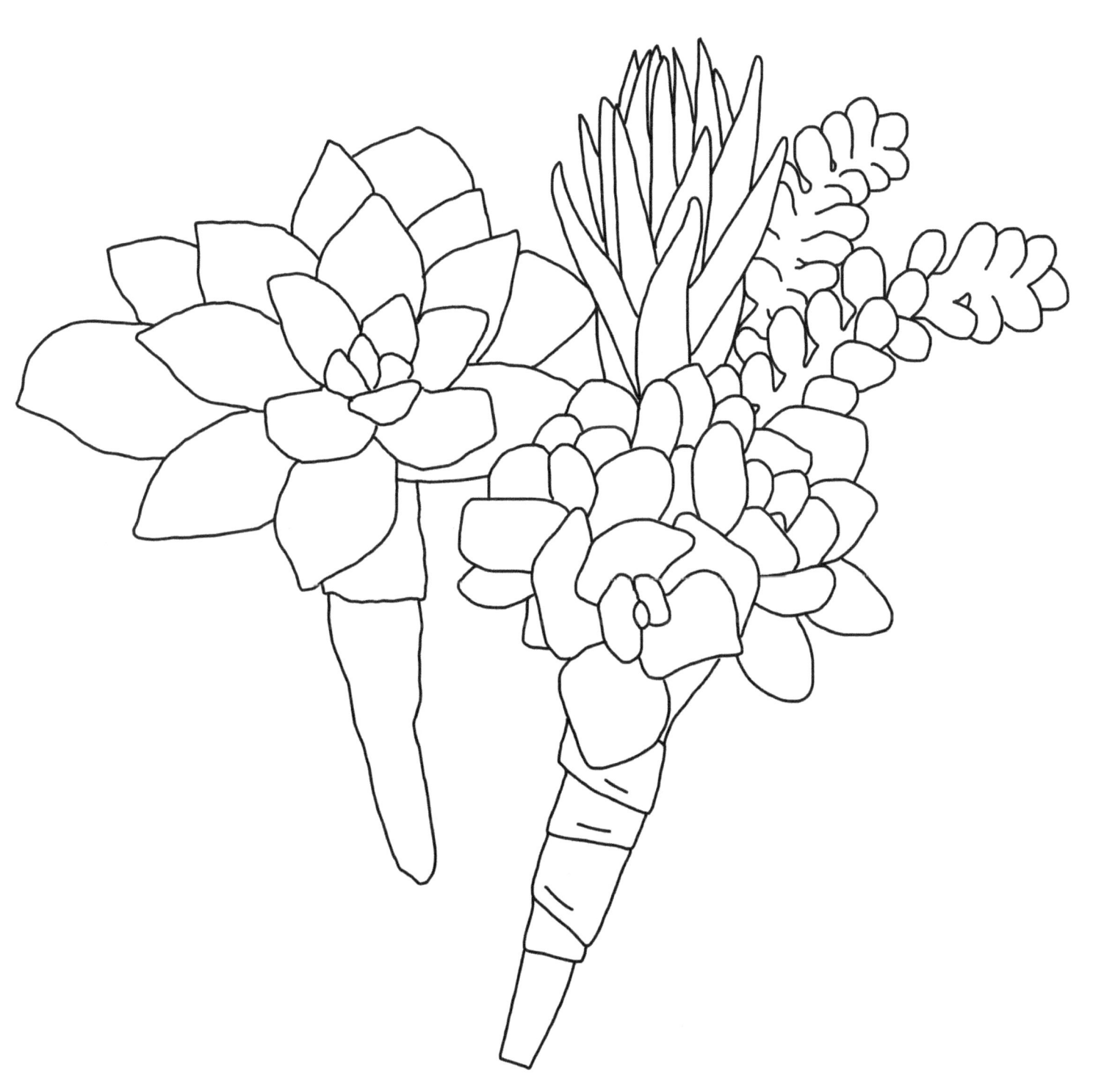

Your Love Lifts Me Up!

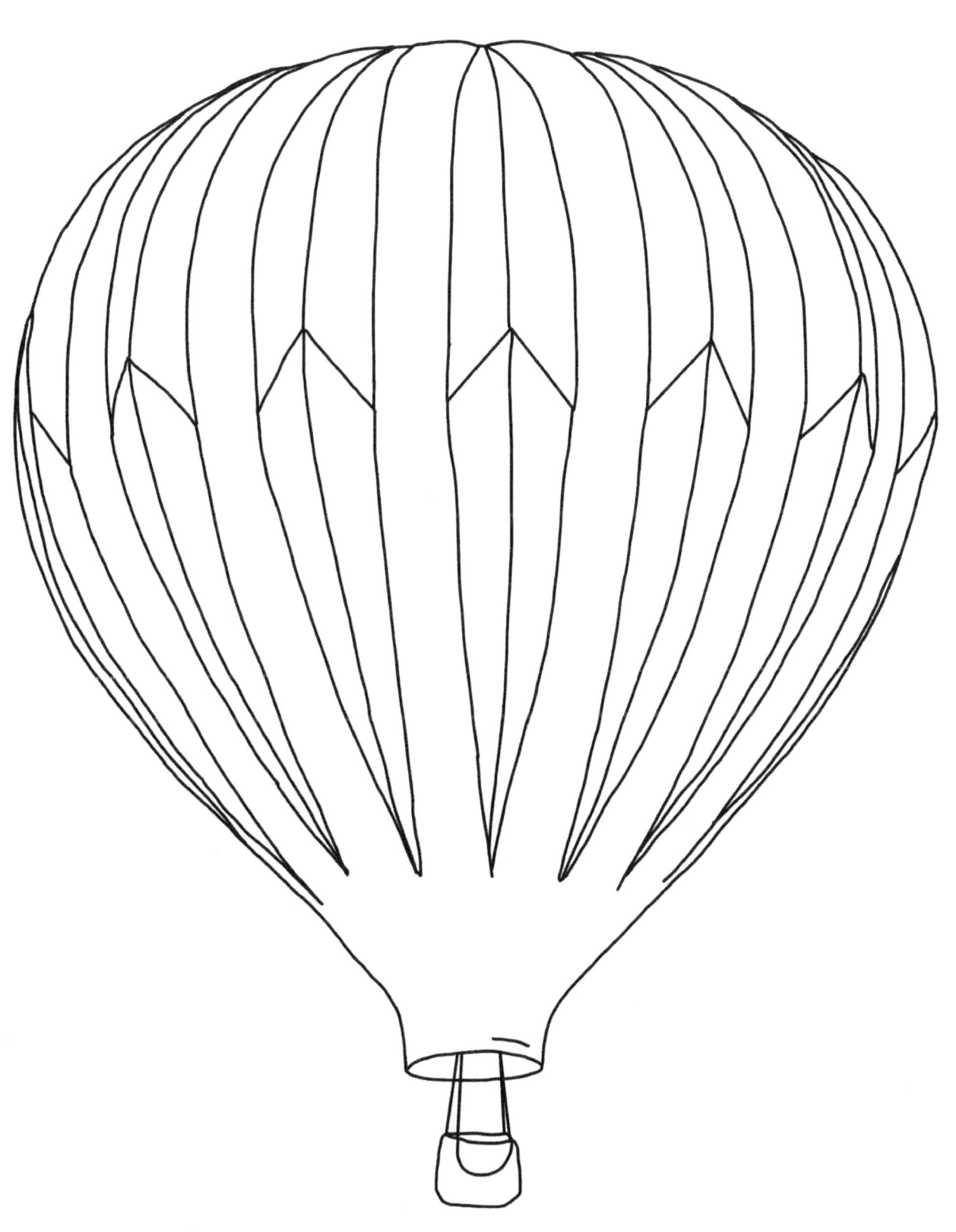

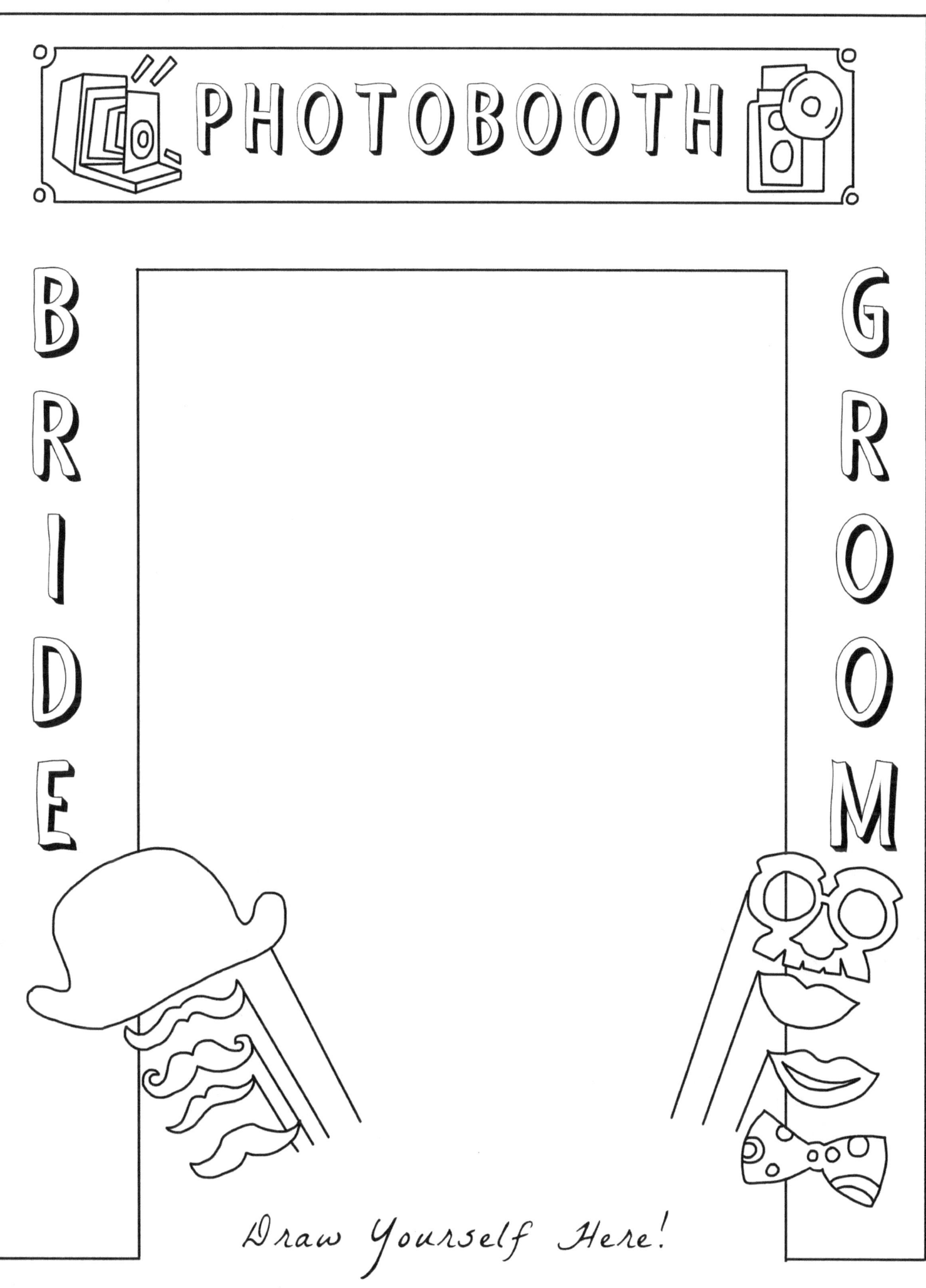

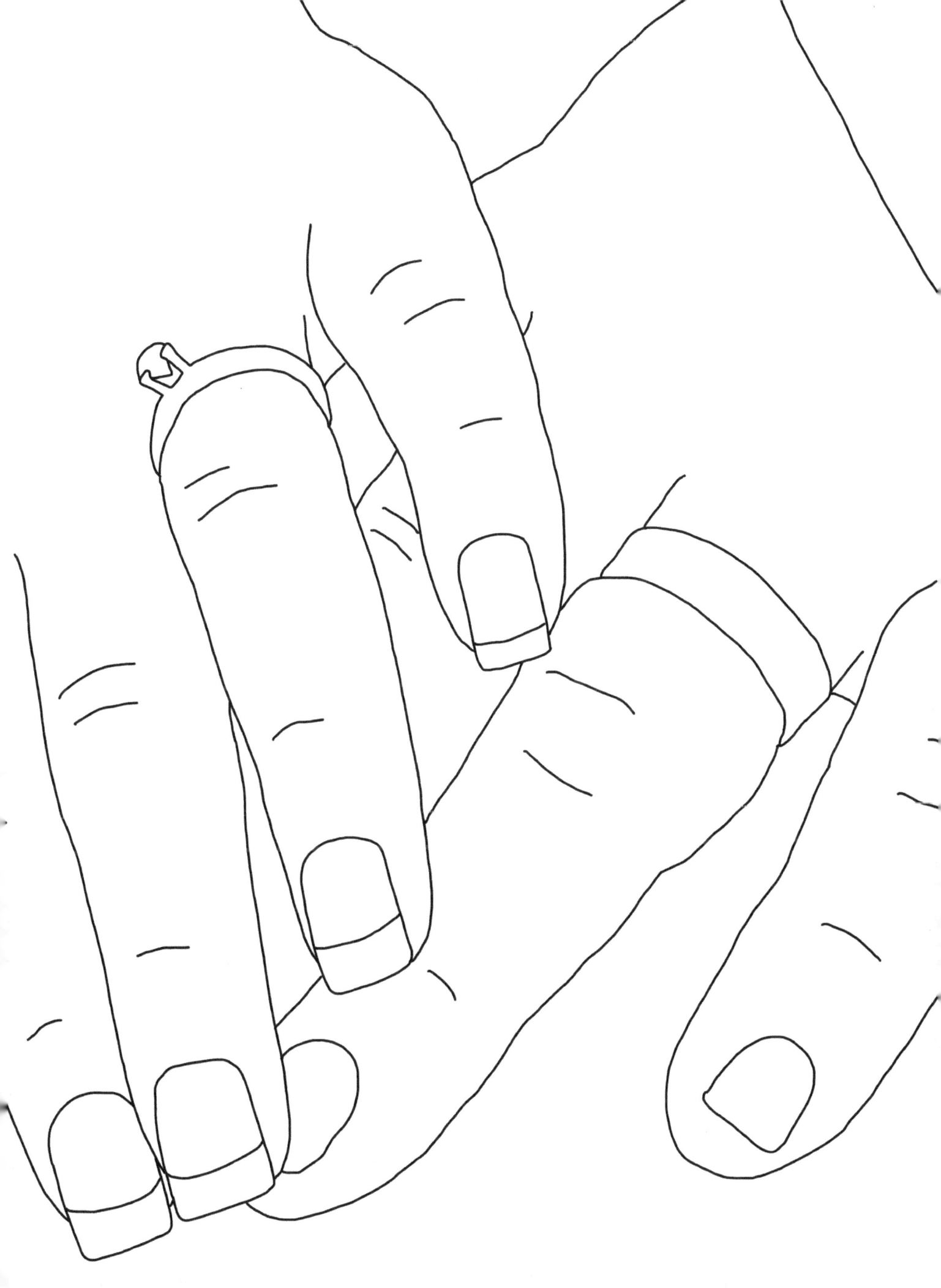

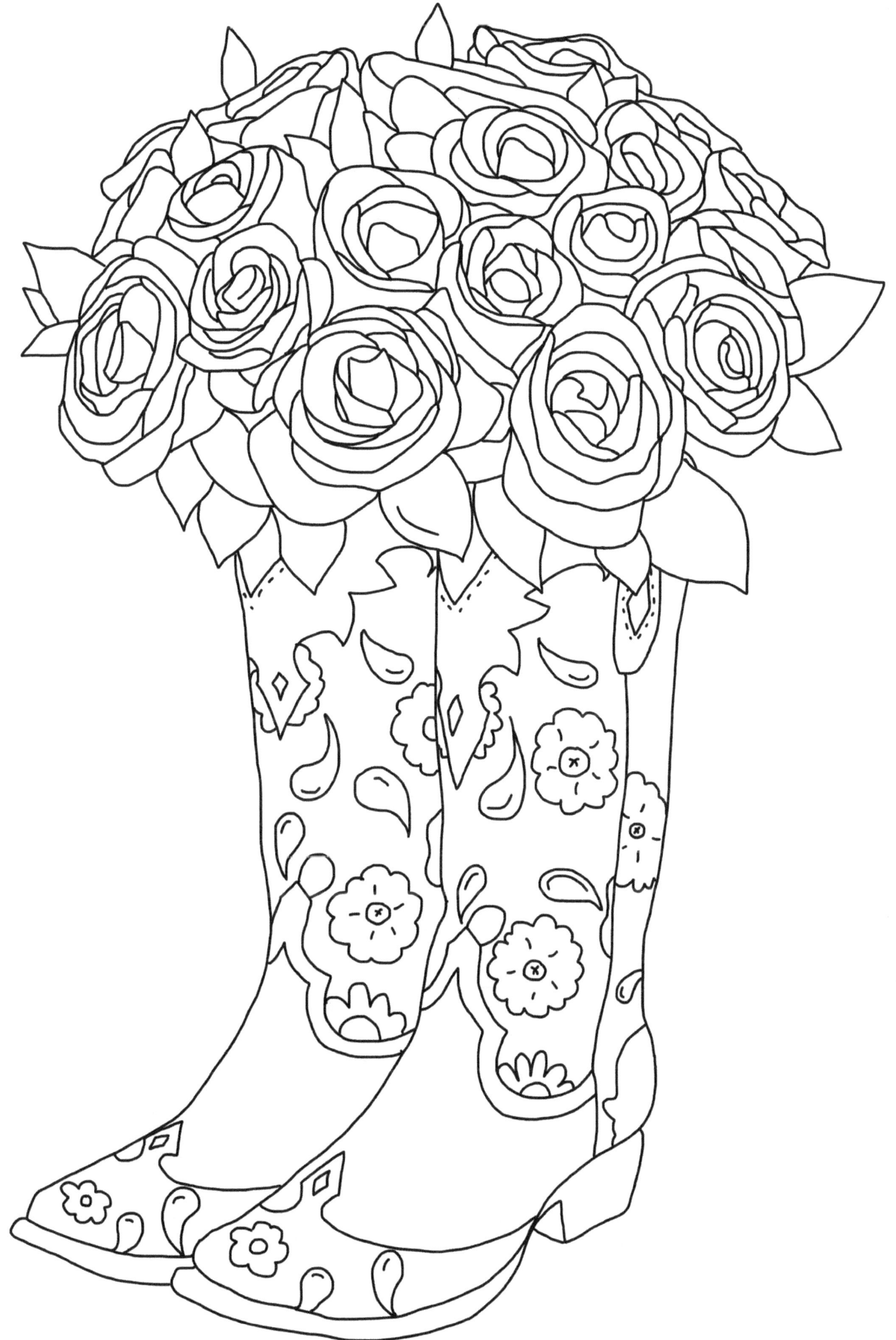

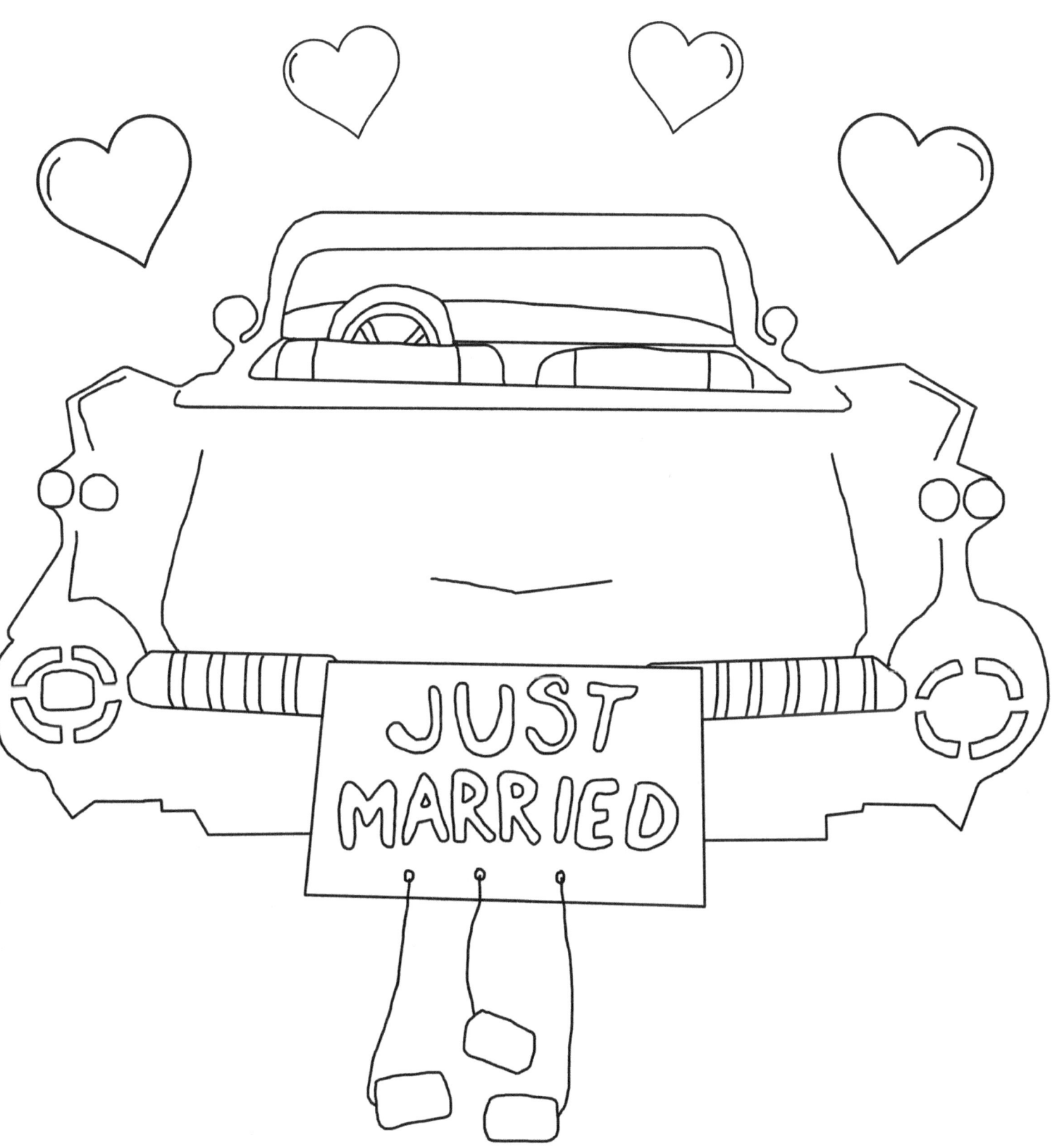

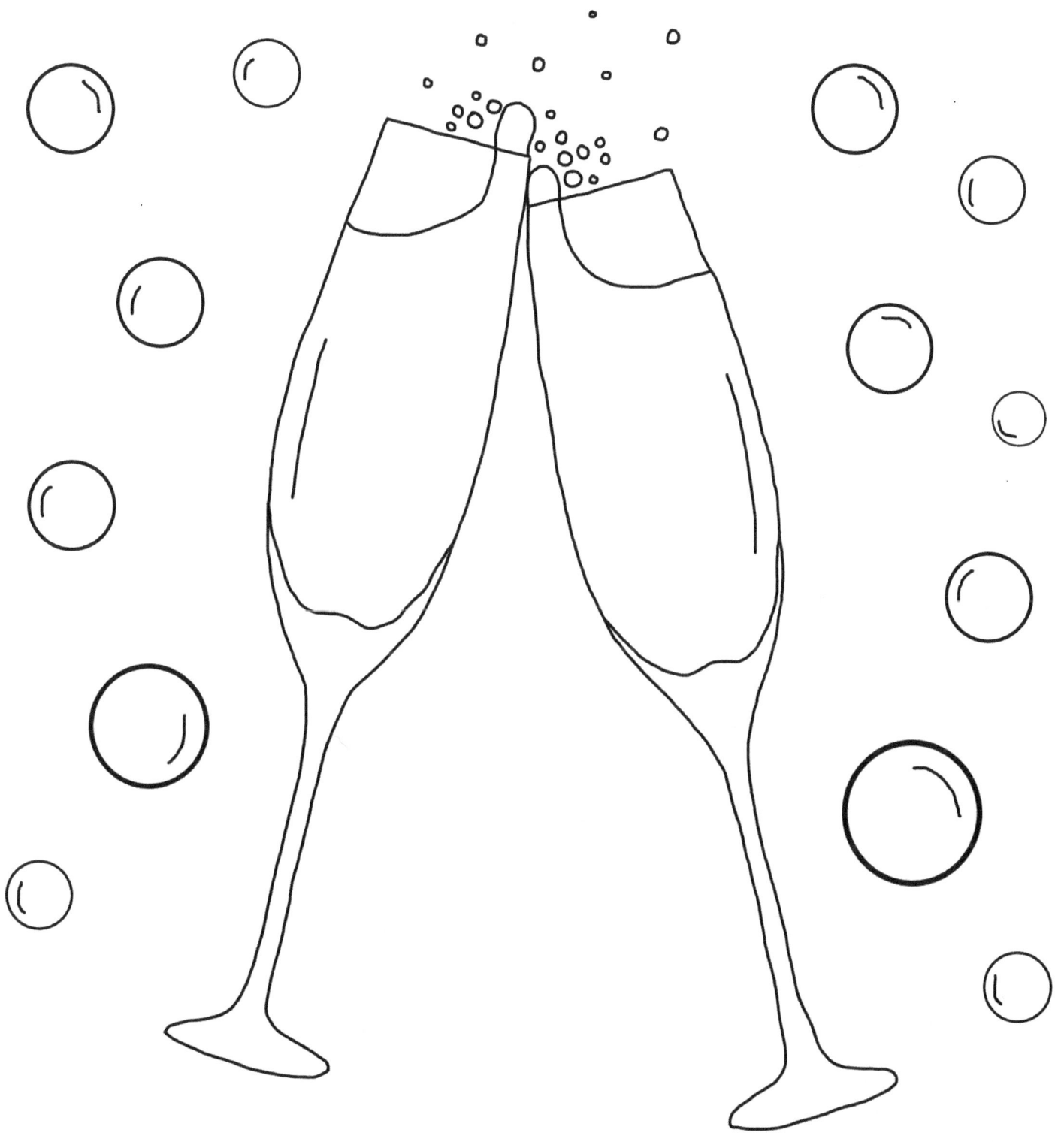

Congratulations!

Thank you for allowing me to be a part of your wedding celebration!

As promised, this coloring book comes complete with a downloadable digital PDF version that you can print and color as many times as you like!

To receive your complimentary PDF version of the Wedding Day Celebration Coloring Book, please follow these instructions:

Step 1
Visit www.curiouscustom.com/weddingdownload

Step 2
Enter the guest password: THANKYOU

Step 3
Enter your email address and the PDF will be emailed to you instantly!

Step 4
Print the PDF version at home or at a local print shop and ENJOY!

 **Would you like to personalize this coloring book for YOUR wedding?**

Add a personalized cover with your names and wedding date, or custom hand-drawn coloring pages based on photographs you provide!

Adding a touch of personalization to this book makes this the perfect wedding favor, bridal shower activity, or even a great addition to your hotel welcome bag!

To add a personalized cover or custom coloring page(s) to this book, please email the artist at monica@curiouscustom.com!

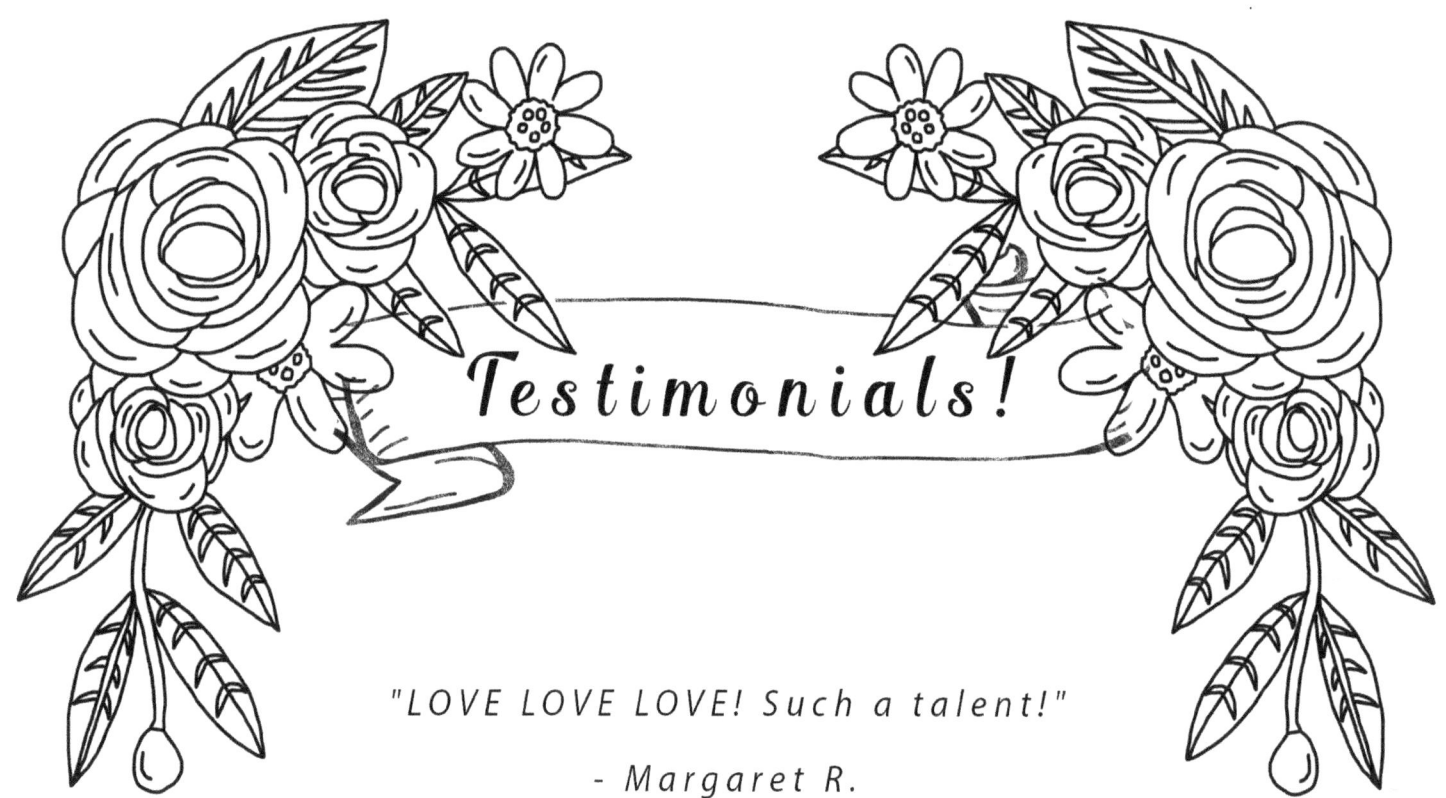

Testimonials!

"LOVE LOVE LOVE! Such a talent!"

- Margaret R.

"I had Monica make a coloring book for my wedding, and our guests LOVED it!! It made such a great wedding favor, and was something most people had never seen before...which at a wedding is tough to pull off!"

- Rachel L.

"I LOVE it! Thanks so much! I can't wait to surprise our guests with it at our rehearsal dinner."

- Taryn D.

"The coloring book was one of the highlights of our wedding weekend! People absolutely loved it!! It felt so personal to have pictures of our parents, bridal party, and even our puppy in the book. So cute and totally worth it!"

-Ted C.

"Love love love it! I am so so happy! So excited!!! Monica is a very talented artist and I am so glad I found her! Can't wait to use this coloring book at my daughter's bridal shower!"

-Sonia D.

"I am so happy we decided to add a custom page to our wedding coloring book! The process was so quick and easy and added such a nice personal touch to our special day. Big hit!"

-Tonya H.

www.ingramcontent.com/pod-product-compliance
Lightning Source LLC
Chambersburg PA
CBHW062209220526
45470CB00009B/2989